CAPITAL INFUSION

Easily Build Your Business Credit Like A Boss

Joany Nuñez
&
Catherine E Storing

April 19th 2022
Boston, MA

CAPITAL INFUSION
Easily Build Your Business Credit Like A Boss

Published in Andover, MA by WMS Press
ISBN #9781735644752

For any ordering information or special discounts for bulk purchases, please contact
capitalinfusionbook@gmail.com

CAPITAL INFUSION
Easily Build Your Business Credit Like A Boss

By WMS Press
1st edition, April, 2022
Printed in The United States

TABLE OF CONTENTS

DEDICATION

We dedicate this book to EVERY aspiring and already established entrepreneur. We, like you, love to learn and for our messages to reach the ends of the world.
Use these tools to grow your business, to help others and to reach your dreams.
We cannot wait to see how you turn our guidance into greatness.
Here's to you building business credit like a boss!

INTRO

This is the VERY book we needed fifteen years ago, ten years ago, five years ago, two years ago, one year ago in order to build business credit for the different businesses we have started over the years.

You might agree that most if not ALL the building business credit steps can be found FREE on the internet. However, the order and strategies to implement such steps are nowhere to be found. At least not in the way we are teaching them here.

We decided to combine Joany's building credit knowledge with Catherine's teaching expertise to bring you an easy to follow, almost paint by number process you can follow even if you are not a techie or are new to the business world.

With this guide, if you follow ALL the steps you should be able to swiftly establish business credit.

Enjoy the process, yes, it is a process. It is not something you can do in a week (trust me we tried). There are steps that require waiting, but don't worry, we will tell you what to do while you wait for all the elements necessary to build your business' credit.

Without further ado, let's get started.

SECTION 1

The Importance of Building Business Credit

What is business credit?

According to Nav.Com (more on them later).

Business credit is a company's ability to buy something now and pay for it later. By establishing a good business credit score, it may make it easier to borrow money when your company needs it.

Imagine being able to pay for all your business needs without having to use your own personal credit card or cash? It is more than possible.

Things you can do with business credit:

Get a business loan, line of credit, grants, credit cards with reward points, extra time to pay for invoices and MUCH more.

Thanks for picking up a copy of our book, Capital Infusion.

We decided to write this book for new and not so new entrepreneurs that desire to build their businesses, a brand and/or to help as many people as possible. Doing all of that takes more than one person, dedication time and the ability to pay for expenses while the business grows and the brand is established.

29 % of businesses go out of business because they run out of capital. Do you know why? Due to lack of funds or capital to pay their employees, sub-contractors and recurring bills.

And only 78.5% of small businesses survive their first year in business (based on Jan 2022 article on fortunly.com)

Imagine if your business had all the funding needed to operate daily and those funds did not have to come from your personal bank account. Amazing right? Well, as you will discover in this guide, it is not only possible but it is the responsible thing to do. As a business owner, when you structure your business the proper way you open a wide range of resources, tools and benefits for your business. One of those benefits is obtaining access to loans, lines of credits, grants and business credit cards.

When Catherine started her 2nd business in 2014, a clothing line, she thought she had to fund the entire operation herself. When her funds dried up, so did her dreams of having a clothing line. Had she known that establishing business credit was the solution to her cash flow problems she wouldn't have had to file her dreams away.

Catherine could have paid for professional samples, trips to source fabric, and check out international manufacturing options in the Caribbean. All those would have been legitimate business expenses. Who knows, she could have found grants for emerging minority women owned businesses. The possibilities could have been endless, but instead, she quit way before she started.

We don't want that to be your story. Your business idea/concept deserves a real chance to 'make it.'

Whether you are new to the entrepreneurial world or have been around the block a few times, building business credit will open doors you might not be able to open with your personal credit or funds (neither should you want to).

The following pages contain ALL the steps necessary to establish business credit. There is a reason for the way each step is laid out. Follow the guide, take advantage of each resource, tool and nugget. These are the VERY steps we wish we had when we first got started years ago.

If you dedicate at least an hour a day to establishing and building your business' credit you should begin the setup process within weeks.

The most important part is to begin and to see the process through. We will be cheering you on EVERY step of the way.

Should you need extra help, head to the end of the book for more resources and hands on help.

In the meantime, here's to your eminent success and business growth,

Joany Nuñez and Catherine Storing

SECTION 2

Following you will see ALL the steps needed to begin building business credit. Now, please be sure to follow the steps in the order we have outlined for you. There's a reason for the outline. Afterwards, you will be happy with your building business credit results.

STEP 1. Pick a Business Name that Can Grow With You

Your business name should not be too specific, or just named after one product or service you offer. For example one of my businesses was called Writing Made Simple - a great name but within a year I expanded my business and my services. The name was limited and no longer fit my new offerings.

Think of a name that helps your audience see you as an expert and also for financial institutions to take you seriously.

Whatever you do, DO NOT USE your name.

My Potential Business Name Are:

_____

_____

_____

_____

_____

_____

_____

_____

_____

_____

STEP 2. Name Availability

My Business Name is: _____

Once you have your name picked up, do a web search to verify your business name is available with the secretary state office of your state.

For example, the web address for the state of Massachusetts is below: https://corp.sec.state.ma.us/corpweb/CorpSearch/CorpSearch.aspx

Secretary of State of Florida: https://dos.myflorida.com/sunbiz/search/

You can also use the platform: http://checkname.com/ to verify that your business name is available for social media platforms like IG, Facebook, Twitter, Pinterest etc.

STEP 3. Meet with An Accountant/Tax Specialist

My Accountant/Tax Professional is: _____

Contact Information: _____

_____

The reason we advise you to meet with an accountant or tax specialist is because many people choose the wrong entity when they start their businesses. And by many people we are talking about ourselves. Catherine had a business for over a decade under the wrong entity. All those years she could have built business credit.

Look at Joany, once she set up her business entity the correct way she was building business credit within 30- days. LITERALLY.

We both have LLCs but we cannot advise that is the best or correct entity for you. A professional (more than likely this is an out of pocket expense you will incur) should review your current financial situation and will advise you accordingly.

Here are some professionals we recommend:

Massachusetts
New England Tax Services Inc,
https://www.newenglandtaxservices.com/aboutus

National:
Prime Corporate Services
https://ercspecialists.com/

STEP 4. Obtain a Business Mailing Address

My Business Physical Address is:

The next step is to get a business address. Do not use your home nor a PO box as a business address. There are many reasons not to; the most important one is separating your personal life from your business. You wouldn't want the ENTIRE internet to have your home address. Would you?

It also doesn't look professional when it comes to opening a bank account for your business.

Now the fun part, finding an address or a virtual office solution (in case you want more services). You can obtain a virtual address with sites like, Regus: https://www.regus.com/en-us/virtual-offices

Look at their services and choose the one that better suits your needs. (As of this printing, you can get a virtual business address in Massachusetts for as little as $46.00 and it goes as high as $90.00).

| Options | What's included | Virtual office services | Global locations | FAQs | BUY NOW |

Business address	Virtual Offices	Virtual Office Plus
Establish a professional business address for your company in a prime location.	Build an instant presence wherever you need to be, at prime business locations.	Our most comprehensive package: all our virtual office services plus workspace access.
	Features:	
Features:	✓ Thousands of locations	Features:
✓ A base for your business	✓ Use of global business lounges	✓ Use of business lounge network
✓ Use on official documentation	✓ Phone answering available	✓ Daily use of meeting room
✓ Have mail sent there		✓ 5 days' office or desk space per month
Buy now →	Buy now →	Buy now →

Once you have chosen the service you want, search for the location you would like your business to be in. (Think of practicalities like being able to pick up mail on a regular basis).

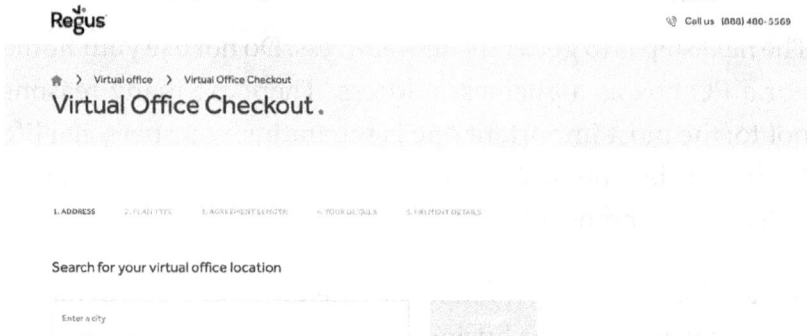

Regus   Call us (888) 460-5569

🏠 > Virtual office > Virtual Office Checkout
Virtual Office Checkout .

1. ADDRESS   2. PLAN TYPE   3. AGREEMENT LENGTH   4. YOUR DETAILS   5. PAYMENT DETAILS

Search for your virtual office location

Enter a city

You can also use companies like UPS. Where you can get other services. UPS has offices throughout the US : https://www.theupsstore.com/mailboxes/business-mailboxes

You're busy running your business. Let us take care of your mail, packages and deliveries. When you use mailbox services from The UPS Store, you get convenience, security, professionalism and other services to help you run your business more efficiently.

Here's what you get:

- A street address, not a P.O. Box number
  A street address can provide a professional image for your business.
- 24-hour access*
  Pick up your mail when it's convenient for you. Your mail and packages stay-safe and confidential.
- Package acceptance from all shipping carriers
  We accept packages from all carriers, so you'll never miss a delivery.
- Package and mail receipt notification
  We can text or email you when your mail and packages arrive.*
- Mail holding and forwarding**
  We'll hold your packages in a secure location for pick up at your convenience or forward them to you, wherever you are.
- Call-in MailCheck
  Save time. Save a trip. Call us to find out if you have mail.
- Mail Boxes Etc. Certified Packing Experts®
  Access to our expert staff to help you find the right packing and shipping solutions.

There Are Five Steps To Get A Virtual Mailing Address Set up For Your Business:

1. Step 1: Find a virtual office solution

2. Step 2: Choose a physical location for your mailing address

3. Step 3: Pick & customize the services you need

4. Step 4: Purchase the service

5. Step 5: In case you started your business using your personal address, use the following form to update your business's address. Complete your US Postal Form 1583. Get a copy here: https://about.usps.com/forms/ps1583.pdf

STEP 5. Buy a Website Domain

My Website's Domain is: _____

Having a website solidifies your business presence on the internet and makes you findable.

Choose a name people can recognize, typeable, and as close as possible to your business name.

When you are doing your domain's search, make sure you are READY to purchase it. You don't want your website name to go away, or go up in price. Make the purchase right away.

Whenever possible, buy a .com domain name (easier for your audience to find).

Set up your account (including payment information. Trust me you will buy many more domains as you begin to set up products, services and even other businesses) do this BEFORE you search for your website's domain - that way when you find it you can pull the trigger right away.

You can buy a domain on sites like:

- Godaddy: https://www.godaddy.com/

- Domain.com https://www.domain.com/

- Wix https://www.wix.com/

- Name Cheap https://www.namecheap.com/

- Bluehost https://www.bluehost.com/

There are MANY domain companies, of course the biggest one is Godaddy (the one we have used for many years. We have also used Wix.com).

Once your account is FULLY set up, do a search for the name you would like to purchase. See example below:

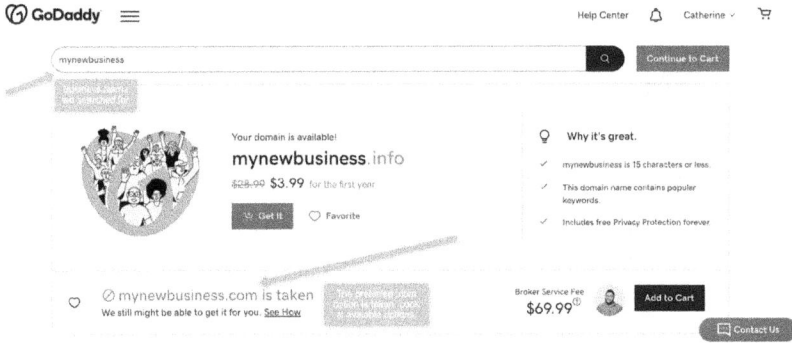

As you can see, the preferred dot com option is taken, you can opt to buy other extensions. The system automatically suggested the .info option as a top alternative. however , it you scroll down, you will see many other extensions available:

Whichever you end up choosing, make sure you buy it for at least a year and if they offer you a discount to buy an extra year, go for it.

Make sure you remove any EXTRA services they may add to your cart (and they usually do) BEFORE you complete your order.

STEP 6. Set Up a Business Email Address

My Business Email address is: _____

This is NOT the time to use free email services like Gmail or Yahoo (Yes, some people still use Yahoo). We have nothing against gmail, we use it ourselves but for business use, you must step it up.

Gmail does have a paid service that is amazing and comes with great perks like extra cloud storage via Google Drive.

Use the following sites to obtain a professional email address paying a small fee monthly or yearly.

1. Google suite: https://workspace.google.com/pricing. html

2. Godaddy: https://www.godaddy.com/email/ professional-business-email

3. IPage: https://www.ipage.com/email/google-workspace

We use G Suite because it is the best tool (in our humble opinion because it is easy to set up, cost effective and has the most included perks).

Every plan includes

Gmail Drive Meet Calendar Chat Jamboard Docs Sheets Slides Keep Sites Forms

MOST POPULAR

Business Starter	Business Standard	Business Plus	Enterprise
$6 USD	$12 USD	$18 USD	Contact sales for pricing
/user/month	/user/month	/user/month	
Get started	Get started	Get started	Contact sales

✓ Custom and secure business email	✓ Custom and secure business email	✓ Custom and secure business email + eDiscovery, retention	✓ Custom and secure business email + eDiscovery, retention, S/MIME encryption
✓ 100 participant video meetings	✓ 150 participant video meetings + recording	✓ 500 participant video meetings + recording, attendance tracking	✓ 500 parti... + recordi... tracking, domain li...
✓ 30 GB cloud storage per user	✓ 2 TB cloud storage per user	✓ 5 TB cloud storage per user	✓ As much storage as you need*
✓ Security and management controls	✓ Security and management controls	✓ Enhanced security and	

Hi there 👋 What brings you to Google Workspace today?

16 |

STEP 7. Obtain A Business Phone Number, (it's Preferred To Choose A Big City Area Code or a 1 800 Number).

My Business Phone Number: _____

Your business must have its own business phone number in order to build business credit. It is easier than you might think to set up a business phone line. You can reach out to your local phone company. However, those services might require you to get a new phone, while the services below will allow you to leverage your existing mobile device.

See below the best services we have found:

1.   Grasshoppers: https://grasshopper.com/

2.   Keap: https://keap.com/features/keap-business-line

3.   Unitel Voice: https://www.unitelvoice.com/

4.   Freedom Voice: https://www.freedomvoice.com/ (this is the service we use) We tried it for 30-days and then it is $9.99/month). It is very easy to use with your existing mobile phone.

Use this special link to sign up for the Freedom Voice business line service: https://bit.ly/freedom-voice-biz-line

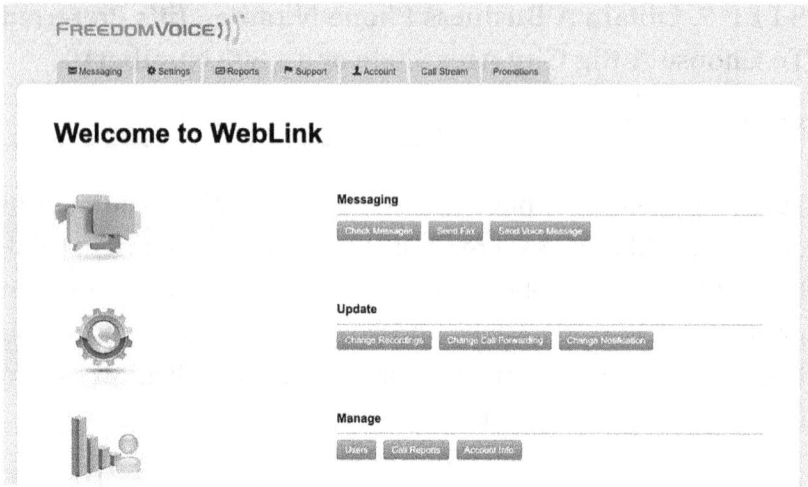

When setting up your phone make sure you ONLY add your voicemail greeting to the screen below. Catherine made a mistake that cost her about 30-days of just voicemail calls (her phone didn't ring).

Catherine called Freedom Voice and they fixed the issue for her. If you have any questions, call them and they will help you set up your forwarding service in no time.

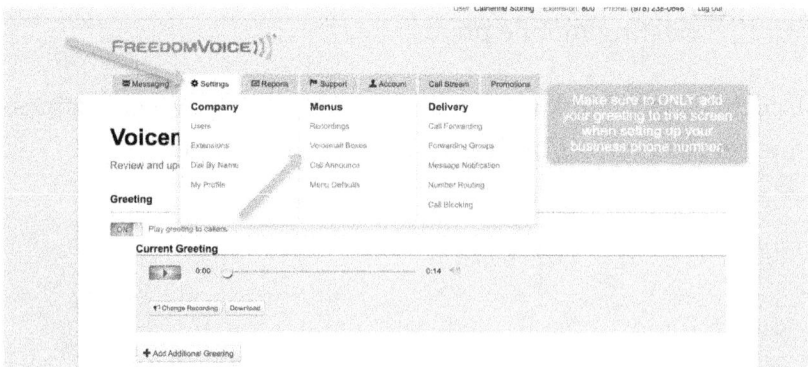

STEP 8. Register Your Phone With 411

Having your phone listed with 411 is a great step towards being recognized as a legitimate corporation. It will also help you be found by banks and other financial institutions.

The process is very simple, head over to: https://www.listyourself.net/ListYourself/

Once you click on the indicated option, complete the following information:

List Yourself! in 411 directory assistance by filling out the form with your address and phone number, then complete the automated validation phone call. You will receive a confirming email in five days after your listing is incorporated into the national 411 directory assistance listings database.

Phone number to list:	United States +1 ⌄	555-555-5555

◉ Residential   ○ Business

Name	Your first name	Last nName
Country	United States	⌄
Street Address	123 Main street	
City, State & Zip	Any tyime	NY 11111
Email Address	businessemail@yourbusinessname.com	
Confirm Email Address	businessemail@yourbusinessname.com	

Validation of Telephone Number to be Listed

◉ Call Me
○ Call Me with a spoken code
○ Call Me, but I have an Autoattendent

so dial extension: _____

Add Listing

After the information is submitted you will see the following confirmation box:

Confirm your number

Any second now, you should receive a call from us on your phone. Please answer your phone when it rings, then listen to the message and dial 9632.
After you dial the confirmation code, please continue to hold until I come back on the phone.

If your phone is not where you are click here and an email will be sent to the address you had entered that will allow you to edit and validate the listing later.

STEP 9. Register Your Business With Your Secretary of State

Date of Registration: _____

This is probably the step you had been waiting to complete, and many new entrepreneurs do this first. This is why that would have been a mistake:

You would have had to set up your new corporation with ALL your personal contact information and that would have meant that later you would have to pay to update the information and thus delaying the entire business credit building process. Besides, ALL the previous steps can be completed within a few days or a week, tops.

We know that it may feel that those are MANY steps, but please know we completed ALL those steps without any guidance and with the wrong providers.

You have the benefit of our mistakes, experience and the fact that we organized the steps in the right order for you. Following our process will help you build business credit FAST!

Here are the steps:

Go to google and type: setup llc _____
(add your state here)

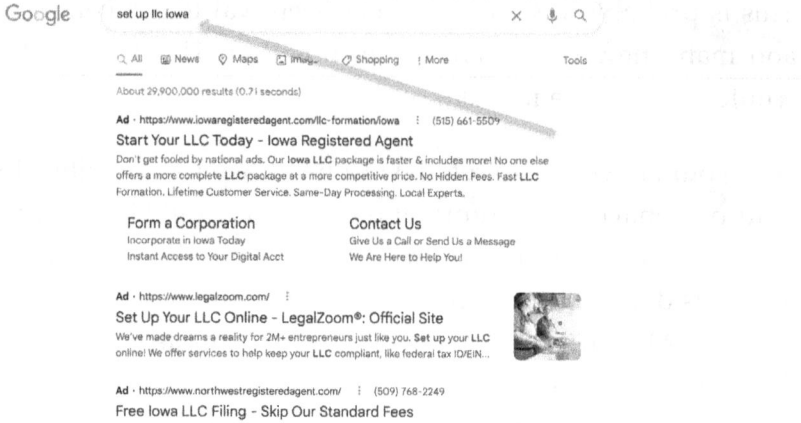

Notice that the first results are ads and do not have the secretary of state web address (most of the time, the address has the .gov extension: (keep scrolling)

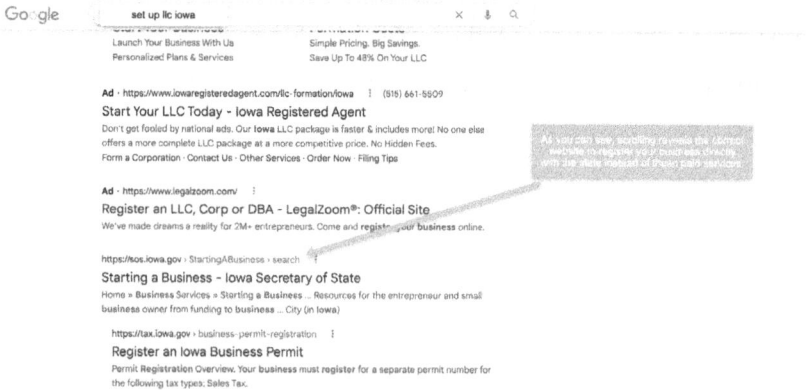

Of course, you can choose to pay to set up your new corporation. The process is not difficult at all, you can choose to go in person to your state's secretary of state office and if you ask questions they will help you with the simple application, you can also ask your accountant to help you (that will cost you of course). We both set up our first LLCs and will pay an accountant with real estate investing experience when we are ready to walk down that path.

Domestic Limited Liability Companies (489)
Domestic Professional Limited Liability Companies (489)

Certificate of Organization [489.201]	$50.00
Amendment to Certificate of Organization [489.202]	$50.00
Restatement of Certificate of Organization [489.202]	$50.00
Articles of Merger [489.1004]	$50.00
Statement of Dissolution [489.702]	$5.00
Statement of Termination [489.702]	$5.00
Statement of Correction [489.206]	$5.00
Application for Reinstatement [489.706]	$5.00
Application for Reservation of Name [489.109]	$10.00
Notice of Transfer of Reservation of Name [489.109]	$10.00
Resolution to Adopt Fictitious Name [489.108]	$5.00
Statement of Change of Registered Office or Agent [489.114]	No Fee
Resignation of Registered Agent [489.115]	No Fee
Biennial Report [489.209]	$60.00
Any Other Document	$5.00

See below the steps to register your business with the secretary of state office (steps directly from the Massachusetts Secretary of State website):

The online form can be found here:
https://www.sec.state.ma.us/cor/corpdf/c156c512dllccert.pdf

In order to form a domestic limited liability company, one or more persons must execute a certificate of organization. The certificate of organization shall set forth in the order provided herein:

1. the federal employer identification number, if available;

2. the name of the limited liability company. The name of the LLC:

    a. must contain the words "limited liability company", "limited company" or the abbreviation L.L.C., L.C., LLC or LC;

    b. may contain the name of a member or manager;

    c. cannot be the same or deceptively similar to the name of any corporation, limited partnership or limited liability company reserved or organized under the laws of the Commonwealth or licensed or registered as a foreign corporation, foreign limited partnership or foreign limited liability company in the Commonwealth, except with the written consent of the corporation, limited partnership or limited liability company.

3. the street address of the office in the Commonwealth at which its records will be maintained;

4. the general character of its business, and if the limited liability company is organized to render a professional service, the service to be rendered, the name and address of each member or manager who will render a service in the Commonwealth, and a statement that the limited liability company will abide by and be subject to the provisions of liability insurance required by M.G.L. Chapter 156C, §65. If the limited liability company is to render a professional service, the certificate of organization shall be accompanied by a certificate of any applicable regulating board that each

member or manager who will render a professional service in the Commonwealth is duly licensed;

5. the latest date of dissolution, if specified;

6. the name and business address of the agent for service of process and the agent's consent either on the certificate or attached thereto;

7. the name and business address, if different from the office location, of each manager, if any; and

8. the name and business address, if different from the office location, of any person in addition to the manager, who is authorized to execute documents to be filed with the Corporations Division, and at least one person shall be named if there are no managers.

The registration may, in addition, include:

9. the name and business address, if different from the office location, of the person(s) authorized to execute, acknowledge, deliver and record any recordable instrument purporting to affect an interest in real property; and

10. any other matters the authorized persons determine to include therein.

The certificate must be signed by the person forming the LLC.

STEP 10. Request Your EIN Number (FREE)

My EIN Number is: _____

Requesting an EIN number is very simple and free when done on the right website (IRS): https://www.irs.gov/businesses/ small-businesses-self-employed/apply-for-an-employer-identification-number-ein-online

---

Apply for an Employer Identification Number (EIN) Online

English | Español | 中文 (简体) | 中文 (繁體) | 한국어 | Русский | Tiếng Việt | Kreyòl ayisyen

Individuals

Businesses and Self-Employed

Small Business and Self-Employed

    Employer ID Numbers

    Business Taxes

    Reporting Information Returns

    Self-Employed

    Starting a Business

    Operating a Business

    Closing a Business

    Industries/Professions

    Small Business Events

    Online Learning

Large Business

Corporations

Partnerships

Hours of Operation

Monday to Friday, 7 a.m. to 10 p.m. Eastern Standard Time.

Step 1: Determine Your Eligibility

- You may apply for an EIN online if your principal business is located in the United States or U.S. Territories.
- The person applying online must have a valid Taxpayer Identification Number (SSN, ITIN, EIN).
- You are limited to one EIN per responsible party per day.
  - The "responsible party" is the person who ultimately owns or controls the entity or who exercises ultimate effective control over the entity. Unless the applicant is a government entity, the responsible party must be an individual (i.e., a natural person), not an entity.

Step 2: Understand the Online Application

- You must complete this application in one session, as you will not be able to save and return at a later time.
- Your session will expire after 15 minutes of inactivity, and you will need to start over.

Step 3: Submit Your Application

- After all validations are done you will get your EIN immediately upon completion. You can then download, save, and print your EIN confirmation notice.

Apply Online Now

Related Topics

- State and Federal Online Business Registration
- Online EIN: Frequently Asked Questions
- Employer ID Numbers
- System Requirements
- Privacy Act Statement and Paperwork Reduction Act Notice
- Businesses with Employees

Five Things to Know about the Employer Identification Number YouTube Video

Click on the blue Apply Online Now Button and start the process:

Once you have chosen the correct entity, and click continue:

Once you have chosen the number of members and the state, click continue to confirm your selections:

Click continue to choose why you are requesting an EIN number

After you have selected: *started a new business*, click continue:

IRS.gov

EIN Assistant

| Your Progress: | 1. Identify ✓ | 2. Authenticate ✓ | 3. Addresses | 4. Details | 5. EIN Confirmation |

Where is the LLC physically located?

* Required fields

The only special characters allowed for street and city are - and /.
Note: Must be a U.S. address. Do not enter a P.O. box. For military addresses click here.

Use the business address you set up for your business. Then click continue

Street * [   ]
City * [   ]
State/U.S. territory * [Select One   ⌄]
ZIP code * [   ]
Phone number * [   ] - [   ] - [   ]

Do you have an address **different** from the above where you want your mail to be sent? *   ○ Yes   ◉ No

Before continuing, please review the information above for typographical errors.

[Continue >>]

Once you have enter the information, click continue:

Help | Apply for New EIN | Exit

IRS.gov

EIN Assistant

| Your Progress: | 1. Identify ✓ | 2. Authenticate ✓ | 3. Addresses ✓ | 4. Details | 5. EIN Confirmation |

Tell us about the LLC.

*Required fields
The only punctuation and special characters allowed are hyphen (-) and ampersand (&).
The legal name may not contain any of the following endings: Corp, Inc, PA.
The trade name may not contain an ending such as 'LLC', 'LC', 'PLLC', 'PA', 'Corp', or 'Inc'.

Complete the name of your business, the county of your business address and the date when you started the LLC. Then click continue.

Legal name of LLC (must match articles of organization, if filed) * [   ]

Trade name/Doing business as (only if different from legal name) [   ]

County where LLC is located * [   ]

State/Territory where LLC is located * [IOWA (IA) ▾]

State/Territory where articles of organization are (or will be) filed * [Select One ▾]

LLC start date * [Select Month ▾] [Year]

Before continuing, please review the information above for typographical errors.

[Continue >>]

Help | Apply for New EIN | Exit

IRS.gov

EIN Assistant

| Your Progress: | 1. Identify ✓ | 2. Authenticate ✓ | 3. Addresses ✓ | 4. Det |

Answer the questions and then click continue

Tell us more about the LLC.

* Required fields

❓ What is Form 720?

Does your business own a highway motor vehicle with a taxable gross weight of 55,000 pounds or more? *   ○ Yes ○ No

Does your business involve gambling/wagering? *   ○ Yes ○ No

Does your business need to file Form 720 (Quarterly Federal Excise Tax Return)? *   ○ Yes ○ No

Does your business sell or manufacture alcohol, tobacco, or firearms? *   ○ Yes ○ No

Do you have, or do you expect to have, any employees who will receive Forms W-2 in the next 12 months? * (Forms W-2 require additional filings with the IRS.)   ○ Yes ○ No

Before continuing, please review the information above.

[Continue >>]

You might have to consult your accountant to answer the questions above. Once you are done click continue.

Pick the description that best describes your business and click next:

IRS.gov

EIN Assistant

| Your Progress: | 1. Identify ✓ | 2. Authenticate ✓ | 3. Addresses ✓ | 4. Details | 5. EIN Confirmation |

What does your business or organization do?

Choose **one** category that best describes your business. Click the underlined links for additional examples for each category.

○ Accommodations
Casino hotel, hotel, or motel.

○ Construction
Building houses/residential structures, building industrial/commercial structures, specialty trade contractors, remodelers, heavy construction contractors, land subdivision contractors, or site preparation contractors.

○ Finance
Banks, sales financing, credit card issuing, mortgage company/broker, securities broker, investment advice, or trust administration.

○ Food Service
Retail fast food, restaurant, bar, coffee shop, catering, or mobile food service.

○ Health Care
Doctor, mental health specialist, hospital, or outpatient care center.

○ Insurance
Insurance company or broker.

○ Manufacturing
Mechanical, physical, or chemical transformation of materials/substances/components into new products, including the assembly of components.

○ Real Estate
Renting or leasing real estate, managing real estate, real estate agent/broker, selling, buying, or renting real estate for others.

○ Rental & Leasing
Rent/lease automobiles, consumer goods, commercial goods, or industrial goods.

○ Retail
Retail store, internet sales (exclusively), direct sales (catalogue, auction house, or selling goods on auction sites.

This is where you tell them what your business is about

○ Social Assistance
Youth services, residential care facility, services for the disabled, relief services.

○ Transportation
Air transportation, rail transportation, water transportation, trucking, passenger transportation support activity for transportation, or delivery/courier service.

○ Warehousing
Operating warehousing or storage facilities for general merchandise, refrigerated goods, or other warehouse products; establishments that provide facilities to store goods but do not sell the goods they handle

○ Wholesale
Wholesale agent/broker, importer, manufacturers' representative, merchant, distributor, or jobber.

○ Other

[<< Back]   [Continue >>]

Once you choose the appropriate selection for your business click continue:

This is the final and MOST important step, make sure you choose: *online letter* (and keep it in a place you can easily find. You will need it often to open bank accounts, request your Duns and Bradstreet number, and many other services/ accounts).

After this step, you will receive a confirmation screen where you will be able to download your brand new EIN number. :)

STEP 11: Getting Paid Using a Business Bank Account & Payment Processors:

Now that you have all your business contact information set up and are "official" with the IRS and your state you can set up your business account - do not forget to bring your LLC certificate, EIN letter and valid picture ID (i.e. passport, driver's license or any other government ID) and a payment processor account with vendors like PayPal, Stripe and/or Square.

Bank Accounts:

Your bank account is one of the most important relationships you MUST nurture. Not all banks are created equal; there are some that are better suited for new small businesses.

We are impartial to credit unions because they tend to require less paperwork to set up and have more products for small businesses. Many have a wide ATM network so very often customers do not have to pay for foreign ATM fees (an amazing benefit for those that travel for business and/or conduct transactions in several states).

Here is the the credit union we recommend:

Navy Federal: https://www.navyfederal.org/
(Does require military service or familial affiliation)

Check out your local credit unions, ask your fellow business owners/friends for recommendations and find out if their services meet your current or future financial needs.

Of course, there are other local banks like Citizens Bank, Enterprise Bank and TD Bank – we recommend these banks because we have banked with them before or do business with them currently; they have products that do not require a monthly minimum balance or a monthly fee.

Other Banks to Check Out:

- Bank of America

- Capital One

- Chase

- PCM

- Santander

Payment Processors:

Now that you have a business bank account you might as well continue to set up payment processing accounts. Why do we recommend you have more than one processing account? Because not everyone uses PayPal, Stripe, QuickBooks or Square? People tend to be loyal to specific companies and the more options you can give your client the faster your invoices will be paid.

Please note that you should not commingle your personal transactions and monies with your business. That is why you should open a new PayPal account for your business and keep your personal PayPal account for personal purchases.

PayPal will ask you for your EIN number, business email address, business phone number and business address to set up your business account.

Make sure to send out invoices or send payments shortly after setting up your business PayPal account. Why? Because when you have a new business PayPal account your first incoming payments will be held for 3-4 weeks. PayPal wants to make sure your customers receive their orders or services and that there are no complaints or charge backs.

After your first payments are released and you receive no complaints or chargebacks PayPal will often set up your account to access funds within 1-2 days.

We are aware that you may have a well-established personal PayPal account, but now, you MUST establish a professional relationship with PayPal. They have an excellent invoicing system, website buttons you can easily add to your website and even send to your clients. The idea is to make it VERY simple and convenient for your clients to take care of their invoices. And probably the best part and most important reason to set up a business PayPal account is that after your account has been established you can apply for a line of credit with PayPal.

Another payment processor we like is Stripe (especially good for small businesses that plan to collect payment for courses on platforms like Teachable and or Thinkific).

Setting up a Stripe account is free (you have to pay transaction fees just like with PayPal). Following you will see the standard fees for each payment processor. Make sure to visit each merchant's website to see up-to-date fees and requirements.

As of this printing, these are the transactions fee for PayPal and Stripe:

PayPal: https://www.paypal.com/us/business
Invoicing: 3.49% + $0.49 per transaction
Standard Debit and Credit Card Transactions: 2.99 %

Stripe: https://stripe.com/pricing
2.9% + $0.30 per successful transaction

Other payment processors:

- CashApp

- QuickBooks

- Square

- Venmo

STEP 12. Build a Website. Starter Pages: Home Page, About Page, Contact Us Page

My Website platform is: _____

Having a website makes you look professional and established. The site does not have to be live, or fully operational, but your business must be searchable.

There are MANY sites that make it super easy to have a website up in no time. Sites like:

Square: https://www.squarespace.com/pricing

Weebly: https://www.weebly.com/pricing

Wix: https://www.wix.com/upgrade/website

Wordpress: https://wordpress.com/pricing/

The platforms we use are SquareSpace and Wix. Both are VERY easy to use, and do not break the bank either (something we wish we knew when we first started our businesses).

Once you have decided which platform you are going to use, head to https://www.fiverr.com/ to find someone to create your starter/simple website for you.

Once you place your order you will be required to provide your login credentials to the website's platform and ALL the information you have for the pages you want the designer to build for you.

The users below are phenomenal and can have your starter website up within just a few days:

1. https://www.fiverr.com/robiul_islam0/do-wix-website-design-and-redesign

2. https://www.fiverr.com/robiul_islam0/do-squarespace-website-design-or-redesign

3. https://www.fiverr.com/aminul_islam33/create-your-squarespace-website-design-or-redesign

4. https://www.fiverr.com/aminul_islam33/create-your-professional-wix-website-design-and-redesign

The pages you should start with are:

1. Home Page

2. About Page

3. Contact Page

Look at other websites for layout ideas of content (<u>DO NOT COPY</u>), use them for inspiration <u>ONLY</u>.

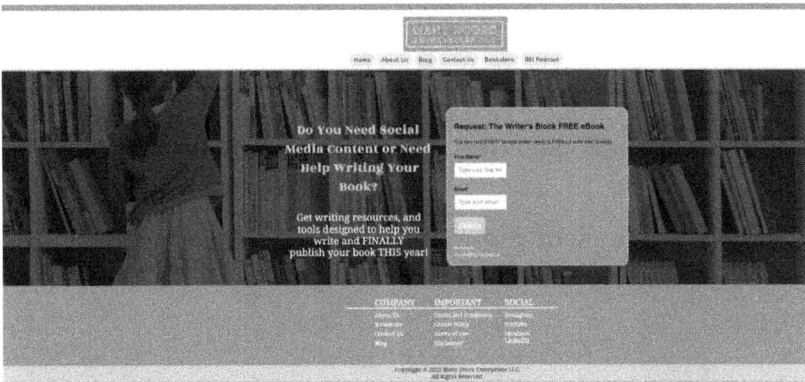

Feel free to visit Catherine's company website for content and layout ideas for your website: https://www.manydoorsenterprises.com/

Check out Joany's website for inspiration and example as well:

https://www.wellnessfirstgen.com/

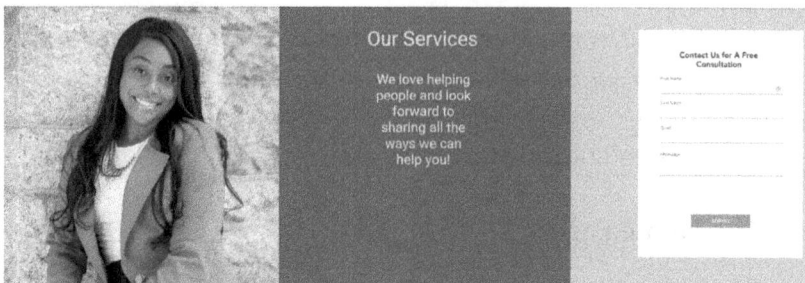

New Website Under Construction

Our Services

We love helping people and look forward to sharing all the ways we can help you!

Contact Us for A Free Consultation

This is not NOT your forever website, your website CAN be updated and beefed up at any moment.

Remember, keep it VERY simple and DO NOT slow down the business credit building process by trying to learn how to build a website when you can have a very simple website built for under $100.

Once you have placed your website's order keep moving to the next step.

While you are waiting for step #16 to come through, you can come back here, and REALLY build and customize your website.

STEP 13. Set Up Social Media Pages/Profiles

This step is VERY important as it will help you be found by your new customers and for organizations like banks and other lenders to verify that you are in fact a business.

For this step start by creating a Business Facebook page and a LinkedIn business page.

* You will create other social media profiles/pages later. For now. These are the most important ones.

All you have to do for now is start the pages, claim your url and keep moving to the next step.

My Linkedin Business Page is:

_____

My Company's Facebook Page is:

_____

My Instagram's Page is:

_____

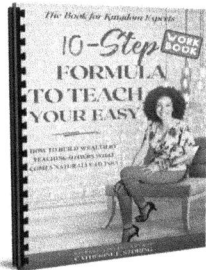

While you are waiting for your Duns and Bradstreet number to be sent to you, you can then fully complete your social media profiles. Need help knowing exactly how to set those pages up you can take advantage of the Teach Your Easy Social Media Workbook here: https://bit.ly/tye-social-workbook

STEP 14: Set Up Your Yelp Account:

Creating and having a Yelp page is a GREAT way to be found online and to also be "confirmed" as a legitimate business by financial institutions.

Begin your process by going to Yelp's Website: https://www.yelp.com/

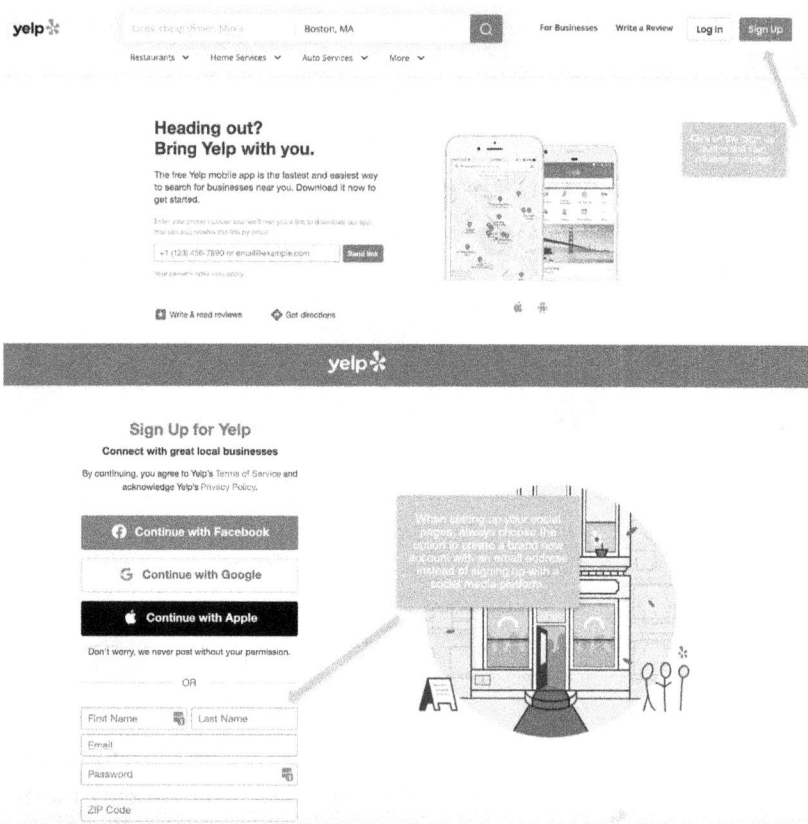

Start by setting up the page, and then again, while you are waiting for your Duns & Bradstreet number you can add services, hours of operation and anything else you may want your clients to know about your business.

STEP 15. Set Up Your Google Business Page

Lots of people search on Google when looking for local and online services/businesses. Creating a Google Business Page is free and is a great way for banks and other organizations to confirm you are in business.

My Google Business Page is: _____

Create your Google business page by going here: https://www. google.com/business/

Click on manage now to begin.

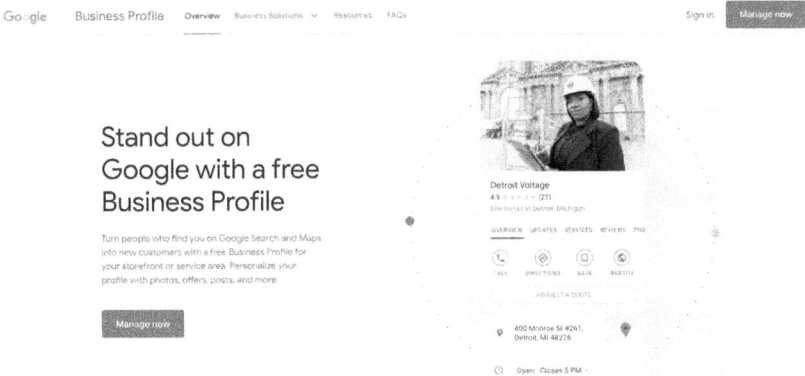

Once you have entered your business's name, hit enter.

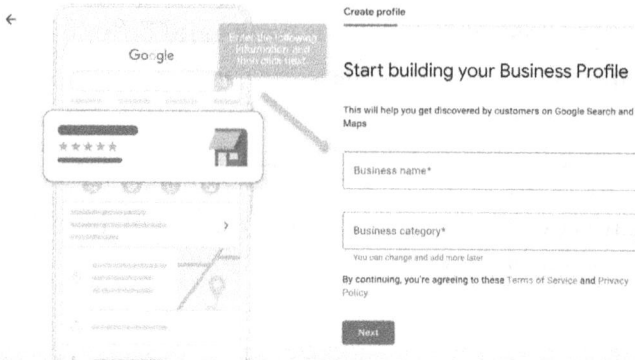

After you have chosen the right category for your business - start typing and you will see many categories - click next:

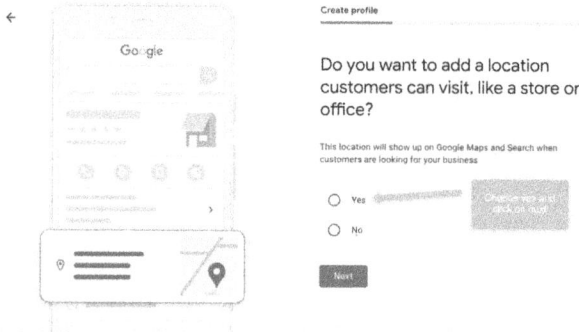

Choose yes and click next.

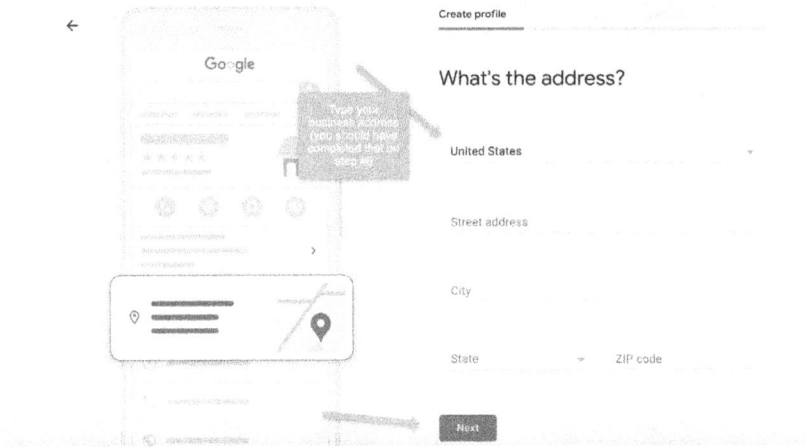

Enter your business's mailing address and then click on next.

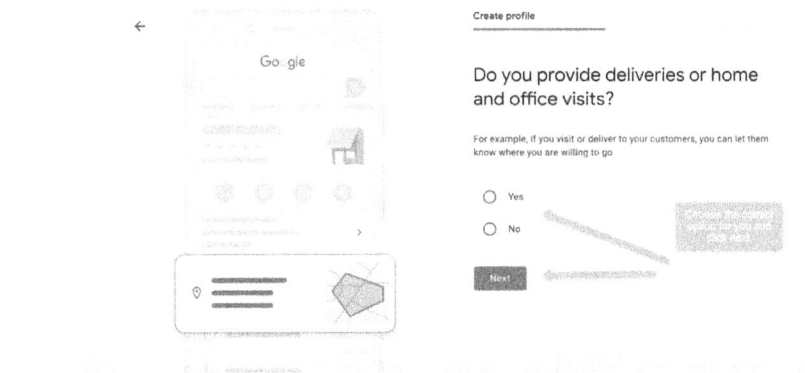

Choose the correct answer for your business and then click next

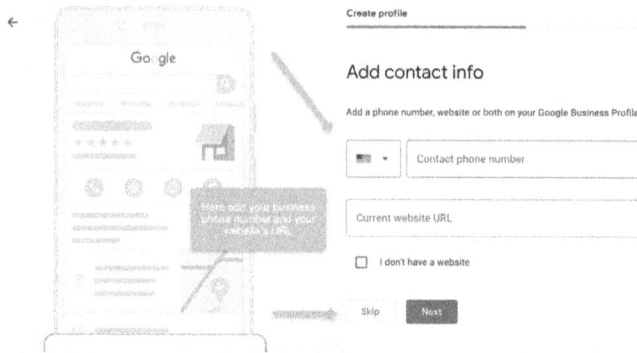

Add your business's phone number and website's URL and then click next.

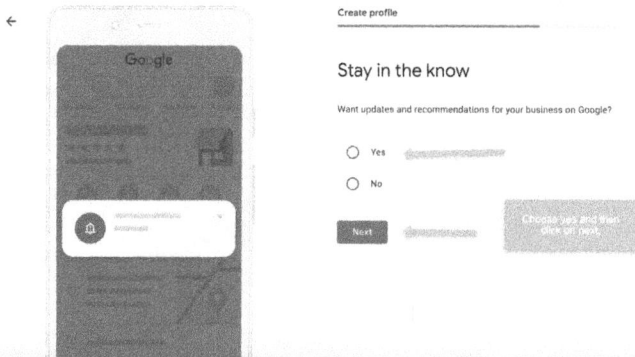

Choose yes (Google sends great recommendations based on your business, niche and the searches you come up on) and then click next.

Enter your business's email address and then click on email. Once you receive the email you will be able to verify your Google Business Account.

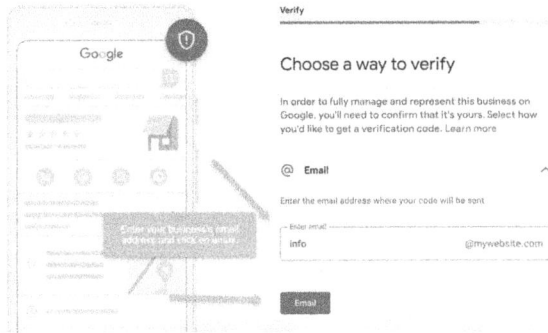

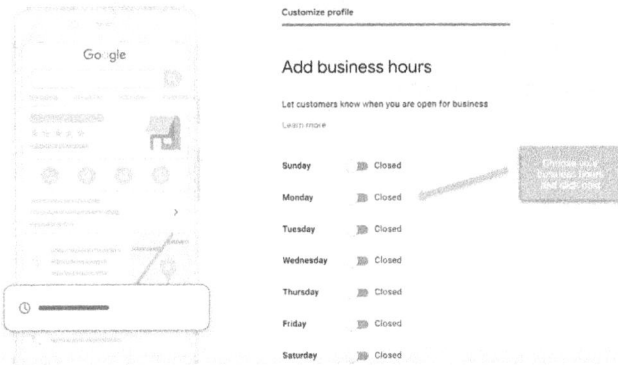

Choose your business hours and then click next.

You will receive an email to confirm your Google Business Page:

Google My Business

Finish verifying your business.

To get your business to show up on Google Search and Maps, we need to send you a unique code to verify that you're associated with this business. This helps protect against unauthorized changes on Google. The code can be sent via phone call, text message, postcard or email.*

We'll send your code right away — it only takes a moment.

Verify now

* Once your Google business page is set up you will have the option to pay to promote your business on Google. (This is an optional paid service)

STEP 16. Request A Duns & Bradstreet

Congratulations! You have created an amazing foundation for your business; depending on how much time and finances you had access to you probably completed the previous steps within several weeks or a month.

Now is time to request your Duns & Bradstreet number. Having a D&B number will open the doors to business capital.

Please note that there are several ways to request a D&B number and those ways change on a regular basis. We will cover two of the ways we recommend and are current as of the time of this book's publishing.

You can obtain a Duns & Bradstreet number free of charge directly from their website https://www.dnb.com/ Please note that because of pandemic backlog, the turnaround time can be 30-days and higher (prior to the pandemic you could obtain a D&B number within a couple of weeks).

When you go to their website, hover over D-U-N-S Number, and then click on Get a D-U-N-S Number.

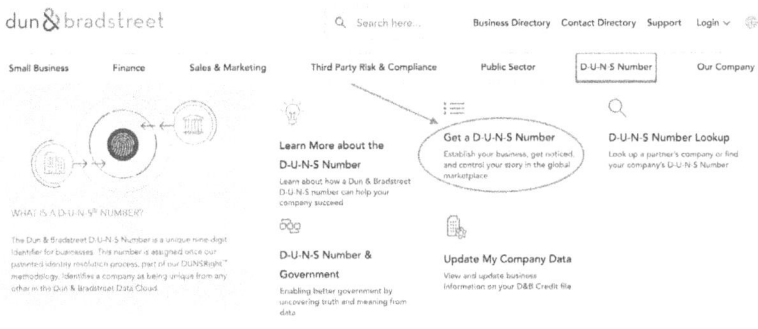

The D-U-N-S Number is used to establish your company's D&B® file, which can help potential partners and lenders learn more about your business, and may also help them make more informed decisions about whether or not to work with you as a client, supplier, or partner.

The first step in creating a new D-U-N-S Number is searching to see whether Dun & Bradstreet has already created one for you.

Primary Reason for
D-U-N-S Number
Registration

✓ Select
I have a U.S. based business
I have a Canada based business
I'm an Apple Developer
I'm a U.S. Government Contractor or Grantee
I need a UFI to Register with the FDA

Choose the option
that best describe
your current situation

Once you select the best option for you click continue. Let's say you selected I am a U.S, Government Contractor or Grantee you will see this screen:

Get a Dun & Bradstreet D-U-N-S® Number

The D-U-N-S Number is used to establish your company's D&B® file, which can help potential partners and lenders learn more about your business, and may also help them make more informed decisions about whether or not to work with you as a client, supplier, or partner.

The first step in creating a new D-U-N-S Number is searching to see whether Dun & Bradstreet has already created one for you.

Primary Reason for
D-U-N-S Number
Registration

I'm a U.S. Government Contractor or Grantee   ∨

Continue

Click continue for the next step: doing so will send you to the following web page: https://fedgov.dnb.com/webform/

(please note that the federal government will no longer require organizations to obtain a D&B number to set up accounts with them so this faster option might not work or be available for you <u>AFTER</u> 4/1/2022).

dun & bradstreet

The reason why we suggest you begin with this option is because it is the FASTEST way to obtain a D&B number (often within 24-48 business hours). We recommend you explore becoming a small business certified business with the federal government. There is no fee to apply (when done directly through the SBA website) and doing so will enable you to apply for government grants and contracts.

You can learn more about small business certification by watching this FREE video presentation here: https://bit.ly/sba-certifications and by also visiting the SBA website: ttps://www.sba.gov/local-assistance/find/

Requesting a D&B number as a government contractor or grantee steps:

After you click submit you will see another screen with a LOT of information. Make sure you read <u>EVERY</u> bit of that screen so you provide the correct information.

Once you have all the information, gather two documents from the list above and then click proceed.

You will see a pop up asking if your business is in the Virgin Islands or not, choose the correct option for you and proceed.

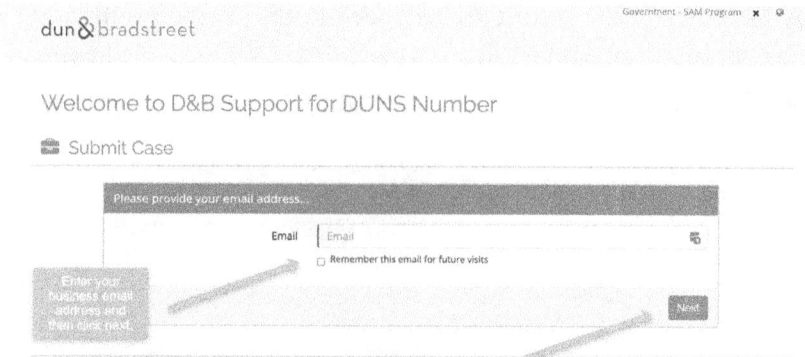

Enter your business email address, review it and then click submit.

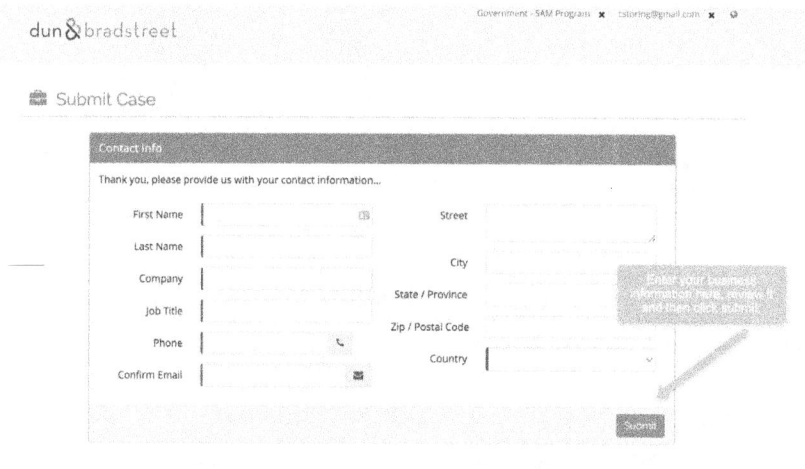

This section is VERY important, carefully read the instructions:

CAPITAL INFUSION

dun & bradstreet

🧳 Submit Case

Create D-U-N-S Number   ●○○○○

In the Full Legal Business Name Field:

- Sole Proprietorships (SP) please use your Full Legal Name (first name, middle initial, and last name).
- Registered Corporations (CORP) please provide the Business Name exactly how it is written on the filing with any included punctuation.

Full Legal Business Name

(For SP) Grant P Smith (or for CORP) Grant's Lawn Company, LLC

DBA / Tradestyle

Company Phone

Please ensure you provide us with your company's physical address (where you keep the books and records for your company). This could be your residence.
DO NOT USE personal mailboxes, P.O. boxes, C/O, or 3rd-party mail sites or your application will be denied.

Business Physical Address

Business Physical Address

DO NOT USE: Personal Mailboxes, PO Boxes, 3rd-Party Mail Sites, Virtual Offices, etc

Unit / Floor / Apt # / Suite

If applicable, please provide Suite Number

Business City

Business State   --None--

Business Postal Code

Enter Zip Code + 4 digits. www.usps.com/zip4/

Business Country   United States

Business Structure / Legal Structure

State of Incorporation   --None--

CEO Name

For sole proprietorships, CEO is the Owner

CEO Title   --None--

Company Website

Home-Based Business?   --None--

Feel free to look up the NAICS code here: https://www.naics.com/search/ here: https://www.osha.gov/data/sic-search or here: https://www.sba.gov/document/support--qualifying-naics-women-owned-small-business-federal-contracting-program

This next section is VERY important (when requesting her Dun & Bradstreet number Catherine made a mistake in this section because she was so excited to FINALLY get to this part).

dun&bradstreet

Submit Case   Case Status Report

Submit Case

« Back

Create D-U-N-S Number: My Business Here

You will need to attach 2 documents to complete this process
- The documents must match the Correct Legal Business Name at the Current Physical Address.
- Do Not Include personal information such as Driver's License, Passport, Social Security, Banking Statements, etc. (See examples of accepted documents below)
- For Sole Proprietorship companies, ensure the documentation contains Your Full Legal Name and Current Physical Address.

Examples of Accepted Documents to Create a New D-U-N-S Number:
- Secretary of State Articles of Incorporation
- Secretary of State receipt of Filing
- Taxpayer Identification Number (TIN) Confirmation Letter
- Employer Identification Number (EIN) Confirmation Letter
- DBA / Assumed Name Certificate Filing
- Lease Agreement
- Mortgage
- Phone or Internet Bill
- Utility Bill
- Homeowners or Renters Insurance
- City or State Tax Permit
- Invoice from a Third Party
- Proof of Insurance

READ all the instructions and make sure to upload ALL your documents on THIS screen (there won't be a chance to upload the second document later).

Once ALL documents have been uploaded click submit.

You will receive an email with your application confirmation (since Catherine made a mistake she had to go back and login by using the same business email address she used for her application and then she submitted her missing document).

Within 24-48 hours you will receive another email with your MUCH anticipated Duns and Bradstreet number 🎉

dun & bradstreet

Dear Catherine,

Thank you for contacting Dun & Bradstreet Customer Service. Your request for a D-U-N-S® Number has been created.

DUNS#:

Company name:

You may search your company in D&B's Business Directory through this link:

Quick story. Catherine applied for a D&B number for a new business the regular way (by not upgrading for their paid service of $229 to obtain a D&B number in about 5-business days).

The process was relatively painless but after waiting for more than 30-days Catherine still did not have a D&B number. She called D&B several times just to realize that there was an issue with the phone number on her account (we know this process is VERY exciting but please make sure you read EVERY screen, read the instructions so you do not enter the wrong information or miss key instructions and also review your contact information).

In the end Catherine ended up applying for a new D&B number as a government contractor or grantee as she planned to obtain a WOSB (women own small business) certification anyway. Finally, after waiting for over 30-days, she received her D&B number within 48-hours.

Requesting Your Duns & Bradstreet Number the regular way:

The D-U-N-S Number is used to establish your company's D&B® file, which can help potential partners and lenders learn more about your business, and may also help them make more informed decisions about whether or not to work with you as a client, supplier, or partner.

The first step in creating a new D-U-N-S Number is searching to see whether Dun & Bradstreet has already created one for you.

Primary Reason for
D-U-N-S Number
Registration

✓ Select
I have a U.S. based business
I have a Canada based business
I'm an Apple Developer
I'm a U.S. Government Contractor or Grantee
I need a UFI to Register with the FDA

Then you have to search for your business (yes, it won't come up but it is part of the process).

Legal Business Name*   Legal Business Name

Street Address 1*   Street Address 1

Street Address 2   Street Address 2

City & Zip Code*   City   Zip Code

State & Country*   State   U.S.

Business Phone   Business Phone

Search for your
business (it won't
come up) but this is a
necessary step

Search

Get a Dun & Bradstreet D-U-N-S® Number and Establish Your Business Credit File

Choose the option that best works for you.
FREE: wait for 30-days plus
PAID: wait 5 biz days

D-U-N-S Number + CreditSignal®	DUNSFile + CreditSignal®	CreditMonitor™
Free	$229	$399/yr
D-U-N-S Number and CreditSignal	Expedited D-U-N-S Number and CreditSignal	Expedited D-U-N-S Number and CreditMonitor
Get a D-U-N-S Number in 30 business days or less	Get a D-U-N-S Number in 5 business days or less†	Get a D-U-N-S Number in 5 business days or less†

You will see this screen pop up asking you to choose the DNB service of your choice.

Then click on Get Started:

Your Business Credit File

D-U-N-S Number + CreditSignal®	DUNSFile + CreditSignal®	CreditMonitor™
Free	$229	$399/yr
D-U-N-S Number and CreditSignal	Expedited D-U-N-S Number and CreditSignal	Expedited D-U-N-S Number and CreditMonitor
Get a D-U-N-S Number in 30 business days or less	Get a D-U-N-S Number in 5 business days or less†	Get a D-U-N-S Number in 5 business days or less†
Register your company for a free D-U-N-S Number and begin the process of building your business credit. This process can take up to 30 business days. We will email you when your D-U-N-S Number has been created.	Get your D-U-N-S Number expedited within 5 business days or less† and take the first step in establishing your business credit file. We will email you when your D-U-N-S Number has been created.	Get your D-U-N-S Number expedited within 5 business days or less and take the first step in establishing your business credit file. We will email you when your D-U-N-S Number has been created.
If you are a business required to register with the U.S. Federal government for contracts or grants, you can receive a D-U-N-S Number within 1 business day. Click Here to learn more.	If you are a business required to register with the U.S. Federal government for contracts or grants, you can receive a D-U-N-S Number within 1 business day. Click Here to learn more.	CreditMonitor gives you valuable insights to help you protect and grow your business by providing you with unlimited monitoring of your business credit file, including your business credit scores and ratings and comparative benchmarking of your scores with your industry's average. Dark Web Monitoring™ helps keep you informed of potential hacking, data breaches, and other criminal activities by monitoring your email address for activity on suspicious areas of the web. You can also monitor one additional business email address for added security.
With CreditSignal, you'll receive free alerts when your D&B® scores and ratings change.*	With CreditSignal, you'll receive free alerts when your D&B® scores and ratings change.*	
	† Process could otherwise take up to 30 business days	† Process could otherwise take up to 30 business days
Get Started	Get Started	Get Started

And continue with the DNB number process.

STEP 17a. Setting Up Tier One Tradeline Accounts (Make sure to read both options)

Now that you have FULLY set up your business (because while you were waiting for your Duns & Bradstreet number you finished ALL the other more in depth steps, right?) you can now start building business credit.

There are three tiers in building business credit. In this section we will discuss two strategies for building business credit within tier one.

For Tier One, we have used these two strategies; they both work. It is really your choice. You can make one big purchase with 2-4 vendors or you can pay smaller amounts for 3-4 months. You can mix and match or try one strategy only.

Strategy 1: In the first tier you'll need to create a relationship with 3-5 of the vendors that are listed shortly (those vendors report to the business credit bureaus).

VERY IMPORTANT: Make your first payment within 5-10 days after you receive your first order.

Instead of setting up new accounts online, call the vendor to create your account, give them your Duns & Bradstreet number and ask to be billed). BEFORE you call them, browse their website so you can write down the item numbers of the products you want to order.

Also, when creating your account, ask them how soon they usually report purchases to business credit bureaus. (if within 30-days you don't see your purchase on your Nav dashboard call the vendor and ask them to report it).

See below the vendors we recommend you make your business credit building purchases:

1. Granger

2. Network Solution

3. Quill

4. Supply Works

5. Uline Advance Auto part instore to apply

6. Zoro online store apply over the phone

These vendors allow you to build business credit in 30-60 days. They'll offer to invoice you; which may fall under net-30, net-60, or 90-days. They report to the three credit agencies: Experian Business, Equifax Business and Dun & Bradstreet. Dun and Bradstreet is the largest reporting agency and has been around the longest. Your Duns & Bradstreet Paydex score is the most important score. Excellent credit business score is between 80-100, you can obtain this by making minimum and on time payments (this means making the payment 5-10 business days BEFORE your due date).

STEP 17b. Tier One Tradeline Accounts Strategy 2

Strategy 2: Setting up Short term (2-4 months) memberships with key business tradeline vendors.

We have been experimenting with different business credit building strategies. One of the strategies is leveraging vendors that specialize in helping new business owners build business credit.

The strategy is the following: establish a short term relationship with key vendors that will report your monthly membership/payments to the business credit bureaus.

Make sure you write down the date you start your membership (we recommend using your notes app or Evernote) and track weekly or every other week your business credit score by using the app Nav.

Set up your tier two accounts in this order:

Nav, Biz Credit Central, and then Creative Analytics.

1. Set Up Your Nav Account:

Head over to: https://bit.ly/nav-cash-infusion

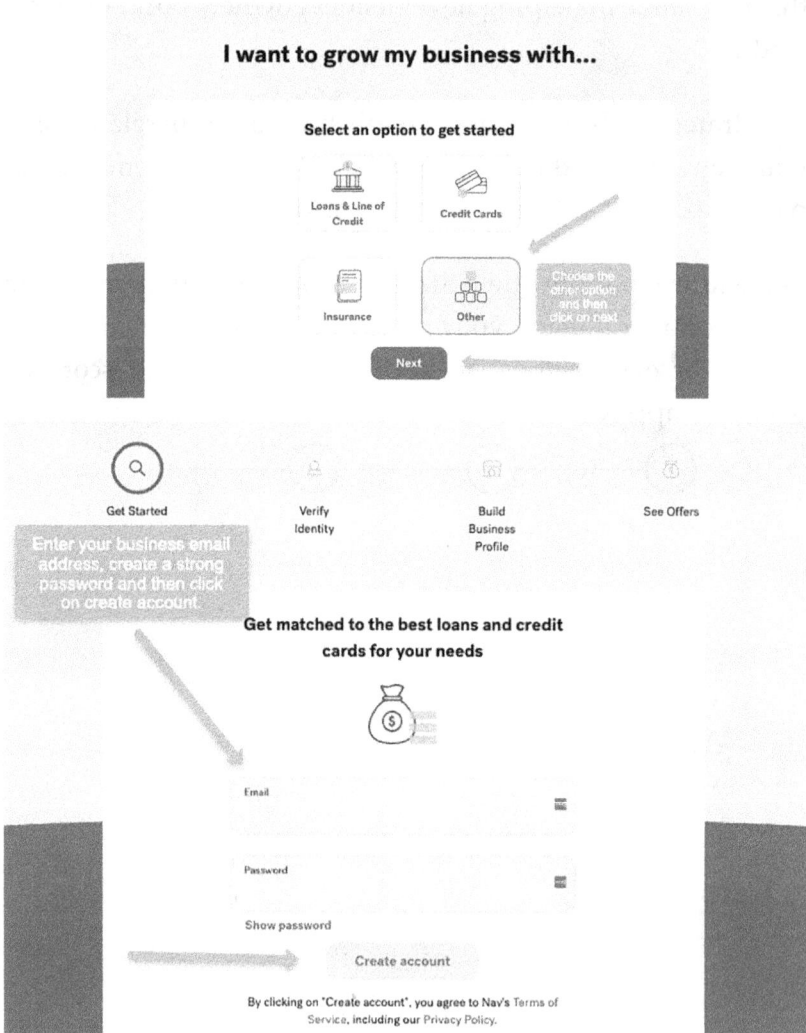

Tool: A strong password generator: https://passwordsgenerator. net/

We recommend you safely keep track of all your online passwords. We use a paid service called Lastpass. It is worth EVERY penny. ($36.00/month).

https://www.lastpass.com/pricing

Verify your personal credit for better recommendations.

First name

Last name

By clicking "I Understand and Agree" I am providing written instructions to Nav under the Fair Credit Reporting Act authorizing Nav to request and obtain my credit report information on a recurring basis to:

- Verify my identity.
- Provide my credit report information to me for review while I have an account with Nav.
- Generate personalized consumer/business financing options for me and/or my business.
- Provide me with ongoing credit monitoring services.

I understand that I may withdraw this authorization at any time by contacting Nav. Additionally, I acknowledge that to the extent that I am using the Nav service to review business financing options, I am a business owner that is personally liable for the business.

I Understand and Agree

Next

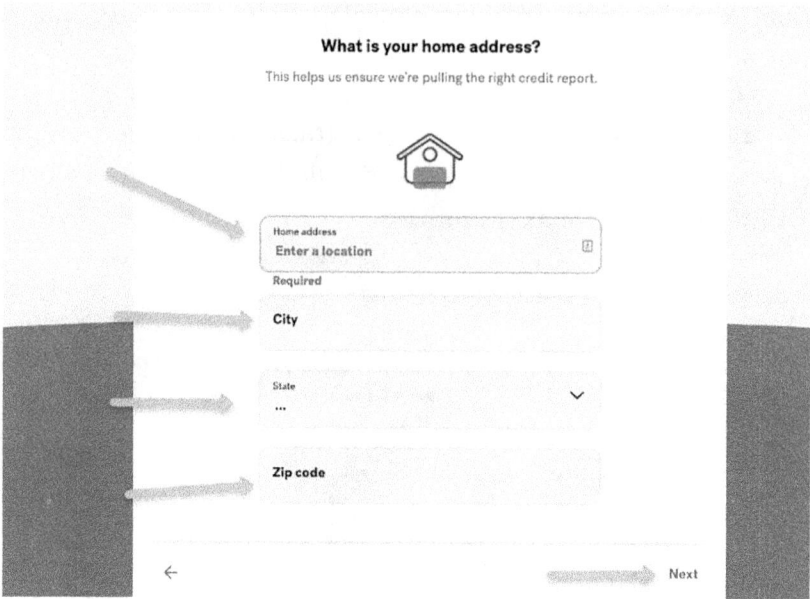

What is your home address?

This helps us ensure we're pulling the right credit report.

Home address
Enter a location
Required

City

State
...

Zip code

← Next

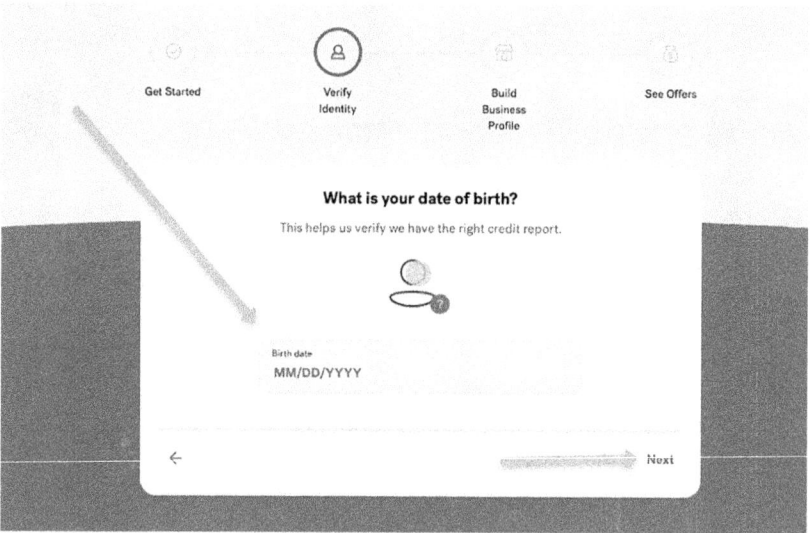

Get Started   Verify Identity   Build Business Profile   See Offers

What is your date of birth?

This helps us verify we have the right credit report.

Birth date
MM/DD/YYYY

← Next

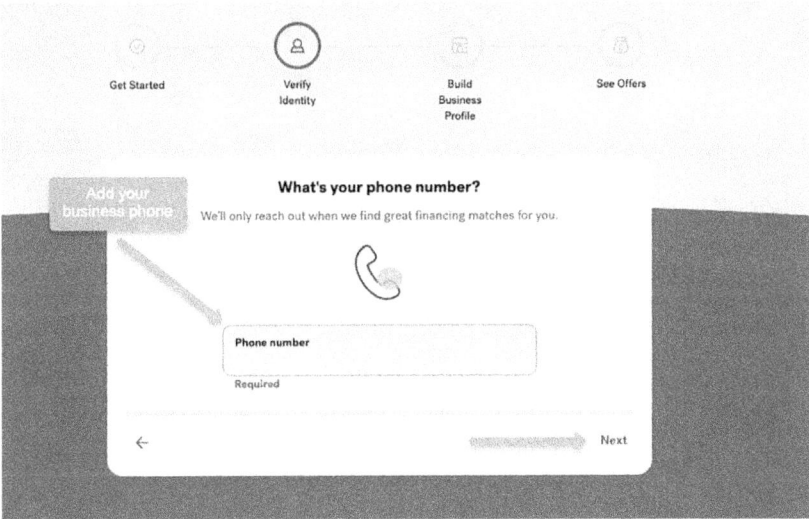

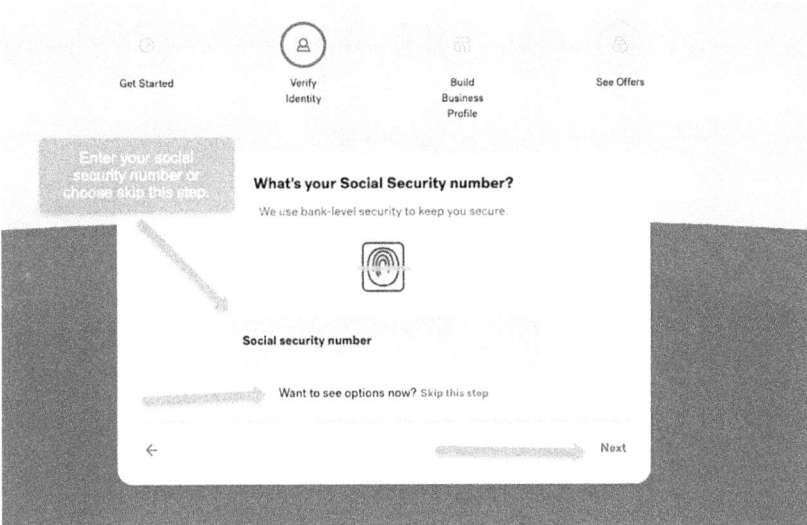

Get Started   Verify Identity   Build Business Profile   See Offers

Review the confirmation details and choose the ones that match you

We've found a match. Confirm these details from your credit report.

1. Which of the following is a current or previous employer? If there is not a matched employer name, please select 'NONE OF THE ABOVE'.

Building your business financing profile

After you choose your business name you will see this window.

Take one minute to see how much money your business can get.

Let's confirm your information to find the best financing options for your business.

See your options

How soon does your business need financing?

This helps us zero in on the best options based on how quickly you need financing.

Choose the option that best describes your credit needs and then click

Right away

Next 3 months

Not looking anytime soon

Next

How much money do you need?

Choose an amount and then click next

This helps us personalize your matches.

✓ Under $20,000
$20,000-$49,999
$50,000-$149,999
$150,000-$249,999
$250,000 and above

←

Next

What do you need money for?

Understanding your need helps us match you to the right offers. In some cases, it can even save you money.

Choose the reason that best describes how you would use the money and then click next.

$

✓ Working capital
Marketing & advertising
Buy inventory and supplies
Debt consolidation
Purchase equipment
Taxes
Business expansion
I'm not sure

← Next

What is your estimated annual revenue?

You'll open up more options based on your estimated annual revenue.

Estimate your projected annual revenue.
Example:
$5,000-$10,000/month = $60k - $120k

$

Annual revenue

Required

← Next

What is your personal credit score?

Your best estimate helps us connect you to the right offers.

Estimated personal credit score

←   Next

How long have you owned this business?

Different types of financing are available based on your time as the owner of your business. Knowing this helps us give you the best matches.

Month
January

Year
2022

←   Next

Hello, Catherine !

Increase your likelihood of being approved for financing by linking your business checking account.

↓ 100% MatchFactor

Search for your bank   Q

Exit ⮕

Share using Finicity

N ▦ Finicity ▦ 🌐

Nav uses Finicity to gather data from Navy Federal Credit Union.

Security and privacy

🔏 Sign-in information is not shared

🔄 Control access to your accounts

🔒 Data sent is encrypted

By pressing **Next**, I agree to Finicity's Terms and conditions and Privacy policy.

Next

| | Alerts | Upgrade | | Many Doors Enterpris... |

Home   Financing   Credit Cards   Cash Flow   Credit Reports   Business Services

Choose to pay monthly or quarterly. Cancel your plan at any time.

🔘 Month   Quarter   Save up to 20%*

*Discount applies only to the first quarter.

Free	Business Manager	Business Boost	Business Loan Builder
$0	$29.99 / month	$39.99 / month	$49.99 / month
More details	More details	More details	More details
● Current plan	Select	Select	Select

Choose between the monthly or quarterly plan (save 20% if you choose this plan).

Choose to pay monthly or quarterly. Cancel your plan at any time.

| | Month | Quarter | Save up to 20%* |

*Discount applies only to the first quarter.

Free	Business Manager	Business Boost	Business Loan Builder
$0	$71.98 / quarter*	$95.98 / quarter*	$119.98 / quarter*
	*First Quarter $89.97/ for each subsequent quarter	*First Quarter $119.97/ for each subsequent quarter	*First Quarter $149.97/ for each subsequent quarter
More details	More details	More details	More details

Thanks for selecting Business Boost

NEW! Build business credit with all major bureaus

Business Boost gives you full business credit reports and scores from the bureaus that matter, PLUS a new positive tradeline with all three bureaus to help you build business credit faster and track your progress. Nav reports your monthly plan payments to the 3 major business bureaus so you can quickly go from credit ghost to lender-ready, and with no risk of negative payment history. Put your business on the fast-track to strong business credit and avoid the capital headaches most business owners face. Nav has already helped over 11,000 business owners establish business credit.

You're almost there! Your upgraded Nav account will have a host of new features.

Welcome to your Business Boost account

Here's what awaits you exclusively with Nav:

This plan comes with tradeline reporting to all 3 business bureaus. In order to report accurately, we need you to mark your business or businesses as owned.

Check the "I own this business" box for each business you own. If you do not select your business, it will **NOT** be reported as a tradeline. In doing so, you are acknowledging that you are an owner of this business and take responsibility for reporting accurate data. If you follow more than one business name for the same business, only one name should be selected.

The day I opened my Nav account is: _____

If funds are limited we recommend you cancel your paid membership after 3-6 months (we strongly recommend you keep this service for at least six-months unless you obtain a Paydex score of 80 and above sooner). Set a reminder on your calendar so you don't forget to cancel at least five-days before renewal. You will still keep your free account. This is why we suggest getting the quarterly plan. Cancel a week before your 2nd payment is due.

If you already have a business credit card, use it to pay for your membership. We recommend Capital One's Spark Business Credit Card. Check out the different options here: https://www.capitalone.com/small-business/credit-cards/ Doing so will count as another trade line. #Winning

2. Once you have set up your Nav Account you can move forward setting up your Biz Credit Central Account: https://bizcreditcentral.com/showmeplans.aspx

Plans & How They Work

Essential Plan $11.95/mo.

An excellent plan for any business that doesn't think it will need consulting time on a regular basis, it includes:

Credit Line You Receive $2,500.00
Net Terms   30 days
Telephone Support Time   - NONE - Billed as you use them!

There are several plans to choose from, the first plan is the one we recommend you start with.

Since this trade line only costs $11.99/month and you can literally borrow money just so it can show on your business credit report, we recommend you keep this paid account longer than 3-6 months …but of course, this decision is totally up to you.

You can also decide to "borrow" a specific amount EVERY month, transfer it to your business checking account (to show activity) and then pay that exact amount back 10-days BEFORE the due date - doing so will show creditors you are a strong business.

(We go more in depth about this strategy at our LIVE Capital Infusion Workshop. For more details click this link: https://bit. ly/capital-infusion-workshop

JOANY NUÑEZ & CATHERINE E STORING

Home FAQs Plans Start Privacy About Members Area

Welcome, !

We're glad to count you as our newest member, and we hope that what we do meets your every expectation and hope. A brief welcoming email was sent to you and should arrive shortly.

We're here to serve you, and if there's ever anything we can do that we're not doing already, please don't hesitate to contact us and let us know. You can find multiple ways to reach us on our About Us page.

So now that you're a member, what would you like to do?

- See How To Set My Company Up For Reporting
- Look Into Becoming An Affiliate Marketer
- Visit The FAQs To Learn More About Your Service
- Go To The Members Home Page
- Go To The Site Home Page

So What Does It Take To Get Started?

There are four easy steps to setting your company up with a guaranteed reporting tradeline:

- **Create a member account** if you aren't already registered - it's free and only takes a minute.
- **Set up a Customer account** - This is for subscription billing.
- **Choose a subscription plan** - Pick the plan that's right for you, and pay your first month's dues.
- **Tell us about your company** - This helps us to report your tradeline every month, so accuracy is important.

That's it! Once done, your company will be included in the very next month's batch report, and you'll receive email confirmation from us about what we report. All of your other membership benefits are accessible from the Members area of our site, including phone and email support services and more.

Show Me Subscription Plans | I'm Already Signed In & Ready To Subscribe | I'm Not A Member Yet - Enroll Me

Set Up Your Customer Account

Your First Name | Last Name

Email Address To Send Updates To

Contact Telephone

City | State - Please Choose- | ZIP Code

Yes, sign me up for the twice-weekly FREE email newsletter, filled with valuable information

Save & Continue

Choose A Credit Plan

Click the title of a plan to view its details and then click the "Pick This Plan" button for the one you'd like to set your company up with.

Esentials Plan $11.95/mo.

An affordable starter plan for any business. It includes:

Reported Credit Limit	$2,500.00
Net Terms	30 days
Telephone Support Time	- NONE - (billed as you use them)

Telephone support and consultation time can be purchased when or if you need it, and we will bill it against your credit line with us on a NET-30 basis.

Pick This Plan

CAPITAL INFUSION

'The Essentials' Plan

Features of this plan:

- Comes with a $2,500.00 credit line.
- Terms are NET-30
- Includes ongoing monthly reporting as long as membership remains active
- No free included phone-based support. Any support hours you use are billed against your credit line and invoiced on a NET-30 basis.

Total of price for enrollment today is **$36.90**, which includes your first month of membership and a one-time account setup fee of $24.95

Clicking "Purchase This Plan" will redirect you to a payment page so enter your credit/debit card information. We do not maintain any information about your credit or debit card. This is maintained by Stripe, who will also be responsible for managing monthly billing of your subscription until or unless you choose to cancel.

$11.95 / month

Purchase This Plan

BIZ CREDIT CENTRAL

Pay BizCreditCentral.com

$36.90

Then $11.95 per month

| One-Time Account Setup Fee | $24.95 |
| Essentials Plan (Billed monthly) | $11.95 |

Make sure to read the ENTIRE page and then click on the green "SUBSCRIBE" button

Powered by stripe   Terms   Privacy

Pay with card

Email: catherine@manydoorsenterprises.com

Card information
1234 1234 1234 1234   VISA
MM / YY   CVC

Name on card

Country or region
United States
ZIP

Save my info for secure 1-click checkout
Pay faster on BizCreditCentral.com and thousands of sites.

Subscribe

By confirming your subscription, you allow BizCreditCentral.com to charge your card for this payment and future payments in accordance with their terms.

There is VERY important information here! Make sure to read EVERY paragraph and then click on the blue "Edit My Company Record" button

Your Subscription Processed Successfully
Thank You

You will receive a receipt via email very shortly. We are excited to have you as our newest member, and we look forward to working with you in the days and months ahead. We are here to help you in any way that we can, and you will be receiving a separate email from us providing you with everything you need to know about what your subscription includes and how you can make the most of it. If there is anything we can do to assist you, please don't hesitate to reach out and let us know. We promise that you have our full attention and support.

A company record has been created for you to complete so that we can start reporting your new tradeline with us on the very next reporting cycle. We generate our report file on the first business day of each month, and you will receive an email from us telling you what will be reported within 48 hours of the report being transmitted. You can also access this information, along with all prior reports, by clicking the "View Bureau Report Information" button located on the Members Home page. **We believe in complete transparency.**

You can start working on setting up your company record right away if you like. We can't process any reporting data on it until you have filled in the required details, so it's important to get this done as soon as possible. You can always update your company's information any time by clicking the "Manage Companies I Have Subscriptions For" button on the Members Home page and selecting your company.

Edit My Company Record   Exit To The Members Home Page

| 79

Manage My Companies

To set up the details of your company, click the "Set Up Company Record" button to enter/update address information, contact information, and general information about your company. When done, click 'Change Reporting Status' and set the company's current status to 'ACTIVE'.

NOTE: Only companies marked with a status of **'ACTIVE'** will be reported in the monthly cycle to the credit bureaus. If your company has a status of 'PENDING' then that means you have either chosen to pause reporting, or you need to complete the setup AND click its "Status" button to change its status to 'ACTIVE'.

To see the current subscription status for this company, or to change billing information, click "View/Edit Subscription".

Company Name	Account No.	Reporting Status			
<My New Company>		PENDING	Set Up/Edit Company Record	Change Reporting Status	View/Edit Subscription

Company Information

Your Company's Acct. No. With Us:

Company Legal Name
Federal Tax # (EIN)   DUNS Number
Year Started 2021
Business Legal Structure — PLEASE CHOOSE —
Describe what your business does and who its customers are
Number part of address   Street name / direction
Suite / Unit
City   State   ZIP Code
Contact Person's Name
Contact Telephone   Contact Email

Save Changes

Manage My Companies

To set up the details of your company, click the "Set Up Company Record" button to enter/update address information, contact information, and general information about your company. When done, click 'Change Reporting Status' and set the company's current status to 'ACTIVE'.

NOTE: Only companies marked with a status of **'ACTIVE'** will be reported in the monthly cycle to the credit bureaus. If your company has a status of 'PENDING' then that means you have either chosen to pause reporting, or you need to complete the setup AND click its "Status" button to change its status to 'ACTIVE'.

To see the current subscription status for this company, or to change billing information, click "View/Edit Subscription".

Company Name	Account No.	Reporting Status			
		PENDING	Set Up/Edit Company Record	Change Reporting Status	View/Edit Subscription

The day I created my Biz Credit Central is: _____

3. Set Your Creative Analytics Account

Go here to set your account: https://bit.ly/creative-analytics-cib

HOME   OUR AGENCY   SOLUTIONS   TELL US ABOUT YOUR DIGITAL PROJECT

CreativeAnalytics

OR CALL US NO

Creative Analytics extends business credit terms to new and established businesses. Creative Analytics Tier 1 accounts are reported to commercial credit reporting agencies to help build credit. To apply for a business credit account, please complete the application below and remit any applicable membership fee - **applicable payments must be received in full before application will be reviewed.** Any fees paid at the time of application are only refundable if your application is denied due to not meeting the stated criteria. A personal guarantee (PG) is not required and no personal credit check is conducted.

Setup your secure account — Register Your Username and Password

Please enter your desired login credentials to access your online account upon approval.

Email *

Please use this email exclusively on all applications or orders placed with our company so that they can be associated with this account.

Username *

Password *

Enter Password   Confirm Password

Strength indicator

Strong (green indicator) password required for security:
- Minimum 8 characters
- Uppercase letter
- Lowercase letter

☑ **Yes, I agree to receive account related emails from Creative Analytics**

We will not sell your information to anyone.
You must proceed with completing the application after this screen and cannot go back/ return to the previous screen.

Legal Business Name *

This must match what is listed in the Dun & Bradstreet database.

Trade Name/DBA (if different than legal name):

Industry *

Accommodation

Entity Type *

Sole Proprietorship

Tax ID (Federal EIN) *

D-U-N-S# *
Enter your Dun & Bradstreet-issued number ONLY — Numeric characters only. *** This is NOT your Federal Tax ID or Employer ID number issued by the IRS ***

Dun & Bradstreet DUNS #

Business Start Date	# of Employees *	Estimated Annual Business Income *
mm/dd/yyyy		

CreativeAnalytics

HOME   OUR AGENCY   SOLUTIONS   TELL US ABOUT YOUR DIGITAL PROJECT

OR CALL US N

Creative Analytics extends business credit terms to new and established businesses. Creative Analytics Tier 1 accounts are reported to commercial credit reporting agencies to help build credit. To apply for a business credit account, please complete the application below and remit any applicable membership fee - **applicable payments must be received in full before application will be reviewed.** Any fees paid at the time of application are only refundable if your application is denied due to not meeting the stated criteria. A personal guarantee (PG) is not required and no personal credit check is conducted

Authorized Representative/Owner *

First   Middle Initial   Last

One individual with significant responsibility for managing the applicant (e.g. CEO, President, CFO, General Partner, Vice President, or Treasurer)

Authorized Representative Title *

Authorized Representative Mobile Phone

If you would like to receive a text SMS message upon application approval in addition to your approval email, please confirm your mobile number. Message and data rates may apply.

Different billing address?

○ Billing address is different than Business Address listed above

How did you hear about us? *

Google/Search Engine

STEP 18. Tier Two TradeLines: Credit Cards

After you have 4-5 tier one accounts set up you can start setting up Tier two TradeLine accounts to continue building business credit. We recommend you wait 30-90 days or once you see at least three of your tier one accounts reported on your business credit report (you can see your current business credit score by logging on your Nav account desktop or app. We HIGHLY recommend you download the app so you can easily check your current business credit score on the fly) and you have a Paydex score of 80 and above. Remember…we recommend you check your business credit at least every other week.

Following this strategy will mitigate your rejection chances when applying to new building business credit accounts. In the meantime, while you wait for your tier one accounts to report you can go back to the steps you did not fully complete before and also you should spend time building rapport with your audience on social media.

See how we consistently add value and connect with our respective audiences by following us on social media:

Catherine's Instagram Page:
https://www.instagram.com/catherinestoring/

Joany's Instagram Page:
https://instagram.com/joanynunez87
https://www.facebook.com/joany.fernandez.9

You can set up 3-5 Tier Two Tradeline accounts with the suggested providers below:

1. Amazon

2. Dell

3. Home Depot

4. Lowes

5. Office Depot

6. Sam's Club

7. Staples

8. Verizon

9. Walmart

10. Wex Fleet Card

Make sure you read <u>ALL</u> the requirements, rules, regulations and fees, BEFORE you apply for your new tier two accounts. Also by looking at the list above, determine which vendor(s) are better aligned with your business so you don't waste your time and or resources opening accounts that you cannot use or do not add value to your company or your life.

Let's say you are in the real estate business and/or need to make home improvement purchases, then both the Lowes and Home Depot accounts will make sense for you. Go to both websites, review the benefits, requirements and fees and determine which card is the best for you and your business.

Home Depot: https://www.homedepot.com/c/Credit_Center

Lowes: https://www.lowes.com/l/Credit

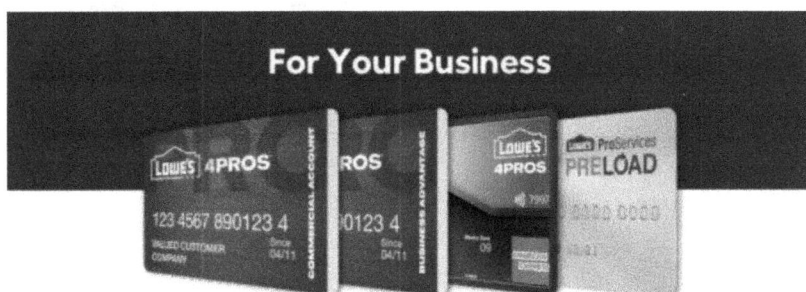

Lowe's Business Credit and PreLoad Card

Advantages that help make it easier for you and your business to get things done for less. All Lowe's Business cardholders receive:

Another business card that will be great for real estate professionals is the Amazon Business American Express Credit Card. As you know you can buy furniture, kitchen appliances, linens and virtually anything to furnish short term rentals like Airbnb: https://www.airbnb.com/ and VRBO: https://www.vrbo.com/

https://www.amazon.com/Amazon-Business-American-Express-Card/

Choose 3% Back or 60 Day Terms

on U.S. purchases at Amazon Business, AWS, Amazon.com and Whole Foods Market.

If you choose to earn rewards, you'll earn 3% Back on the first $120,000 in purchases each calendar year, 1% Back thereafter

$0 Annual Fee

1% Back
On other purchases

2% Back
At U.S. restaurants, U.S. gas stations, and on wireless telephone services purchased directly from U.S. service providers

Earn a **$100 statement credit** after you make $3,000 in purchases on your Card in your first 3 months.

Choose 5% Back or 90 Day Terms

on U.S. purchases at Amazon Business, AWS, Amazon.com and Whole Foods Market with an eligible Prime membership

If you choose to earn rewards, you'll earn 5% Back on the first $120,000 in purchases each calendar year, 1% Back thereafter

$0 Annual Fee

1% Back
On other purchases

2% Back
At U.S. restaurants, U.S. gas stations, and on wireless telephone services purchased directly from U.S. service providers

Earn a **$100 statement credit** after you make $3,000 in purchases on your Card in your first 3 months.

STEP 19. Tier Three TradeLines: Business Credit/ Business Loans

You should start utilizing/leveraging tier three vendors within six months from when you started building business credit. By now you have (hopefully) developed a good relationship with your tier one and tier two vendors and have been making on time payments on your accounts.

Your business credit score should be between 95-100 points at this time. As you know you can find your business credit information by logging on to your Dun & Bradstreet and Nav accounts. At this time, you can apply for major loans from these suggested vendors:

1. AMEX: https://www.americanexpress.com/us/business/business-funding/business-loans/

2. Blue Vine: https://www.bluevine.com/lp6-business-line-of-credit/

3. Citizens: https://www.citizensbank.com/small-business/loans/overview.aspx

4. Navy Federal Credit Union: https://www.navyfederal.org/services/business/loans.html

5. PNC: https://www.pnc.com/en/small-business/borrowing/business-loans.html

6. SBA Loans: https://www.sba.gov/funding-programs/loans

7. Wells Fargo: https://www.wellsfargo.com/biz/business-credit/

Why would you want to procure a business loan? Well depending on your business you might have to buy a commercial vehicle, pay for supplies to fulfill orders, get a commercial space, hire consultants, pay for coaches or training, travel nationally or abroad for certifications and/or conferences, or to make business investments.

Whatever the reason(s) for the business loans, all your hard work building business credit will pay off and allow you to use your personal resources to fund other projects and continue to build your retirement nest egg.

STEP 20. What Happens After You Have Establish Business Credits

Congratulations! You have finished going through the Capital Infusion Workbook. Now you should be on your way to establishing even stronger business credit.

We know that people learn differently and that's why we decided to create a LIVE video version of this guide. Where we go through EVERY step and answer the most frequently asked questions from our students.

Whether you need help with the beginning, the middle or finishing some or ALL of the business credit building steps, this workshop will help you.

Click the link below for more information to attend the next virtual or in person workshop session: https://bit.ly/capital-infusion-workshop

ABOUT THE AUTHORS

Joany Nuñez

Joany Nuñez is a licensed financial expert, advisor, and author with over 7 years of professional experience. Her areas of expertise include retirement planning, wealth management, financial planning, investment strategies, long-term care planning, estate, and trust services, health insurance, homeowners insurance, and other various insurances, debt, and credit-building strategies. Joany is committed to building long-lasting client relationships by maintaining the highest standards of quality, professionalism, and integrity.

She excels in the area of personal finance, and she empowers her clients to take charge of their destiny through proper financial management in order to live a more fulfilled and meaningful life. Due to her Afro-Latina roots, Joany is a fierce advocate for financial literacy among women, Black Americans, and Hispanic and Latin Americans. Empowering and educating are the foundations of her relationships. Through her strong active listening, analytical and accessible nature, she has been able to customize services to bridge the gap between wealth, family dynamics, and the next generation.

Before joining the financial services industry Joany worked in the Healthcare and Benefits industry helping families and individuals find the best coverage that meets their medical needs. After 15years in the Healthcare and Benefits industry, adding financial services to her list of products was the logical decision to make her practice comprehensive.

Joany Nuñez is the CEO of Wellness First Gen, a Licensed Health and Financial Consultant, retirement advisor, and author. She earned a Bachelor's in Healthcare Management at Southern New Hampshire University, Salem, NH. Her book *Capital Infusion* helps to educate small business owners on how to obtain and build small business credit, to help them leverage better financial opportunities as they grow.

About Wellness First Gen

Wellness First Gen is a Financial Consulting Firm, founded by Joany Nunez a Financial Expert. Wellness First Gen primarily focuses on health and financial strategies for individuals, families, and businesses by assisting clients with life's transitions and providing a solid financial plan and guidance in times of change. It provides financial planning products and services, including wealth management, asset management, insurance, annuities, and estate planning.

Connect with Joany online:

https://www.facebook.com/joany.fernandez.9

https://www.instagram.com/joanynunez87/

https://www.wellnessfirstgen.com/

Catherine Storing

Content Monetization Strategist, Amazon Best-Seller and author of 25+ books, creator of 20+ courses, writing coach, Keynote/2-time TEDx Speaker, founder of WMS PRESS, Certified Life Coach, Certified Christian Mentor and woman of faith.

I have been coaching others for more than twenty years (even when I did not know it yet). I never thought my love for words, books, and writing would allow me to pool my expertise and help others to bring out their authentic voice and content to the world.

Today I get to work with experts, authors, speakers, coaches, real estate investors, and entrepreneurs who are willing and ready to serve others with their expertise and talents in a global capacity; however, they know they need to monetize their expertise and need someone that can guide them through the monetization process.

Connect with Catherine online:

Facebook: https://www.facebook.com/catherinestoring/

Instagram: https://www.instagram.com/catherinestoring/

YouTube:https://www.youtube.com/c/CatherineStoring

Website: https://www.manydoorsenterprises.com/

NOTES

_____

_____

_____

_____

_____

_____

_____

_____

_____

_____

_____

_____

---

www.ingramcontent.com/pod-product-compliance
Lightning Source LLC
Chambersburg PA
CBHW071720210326
41597CB00017B/2541